IMAGES
of America

UNION

IMAGES
of America

UNION

Compiled by
David Alan Johnson

ARCADIA

Copyright © 1994 by David Alan Johnson
ISBN 0-7524-0095-9

First published 1994
Reprinted 2000, 2003

Published by Arcadia Publishing,
an imprint of Tempus Publishing Inc.
Portsmouth NH, Charleston SC, Chicago,
San Francisco

Printed in Great Britain

For all general information, contact Arcadia Publishing:
Telephone 843-853-2070
Fax 843-853-0044
E-mail sales@arcadiapublishing.com
For customer service and orders:
Toll-free 1-888-313-2665

Visit us on the Internet at www.arcadiapublishing.com

Contents

Acknowledgments

I would like to thank . . . this is where everyone stops reading.

But a number of individuals have been more than kind to me in this venture, and it would be in extremely bad taste not to mention them. So at the risk of becoming a cliché, and a boring one at that, I simply have to say "Thank you" to: the Union Township Historical Society for allowing me to use their photographs, and especially Mr. Mike Yesenko for his time, his expertise, and his patience; Barbara Grillo of Connecticut Farms Church, who set aside a humid afternoon in July so that I could rummage through the church's photo archives; Lou Giacona, Union Township administrator, for allowing me to use the Township's picture collection; Mrs Jack Zissel, Marguerite Miltner, Millicent Egbert, and Pauline Foster for lending photographs from their collections; Laura Libby, for her help, her suggestions, and sometimes just for staying out of the way; and, finally, to Peter and Carolyn Hammond of Chiswick, West London, who got me into this thing in the first place.

Introduction

"These fragments I have shored against my ruins," a line from T.S. Eliot's *The Waste Land*, kept running through my mind while I was assembling this collection. What else is a photo-history if not fragments of the past that are assembled in an attempt to come to terms with it?

Union began as a small village surrounded by farmland. The founding families came mostly from the vicinity of Branford and Guilford, Connecticut, so they decided to call their new home Connecticut Farms. They bought the land from local natives, the Lenae Lenape of the Minnisink tribe. In the 1660s, land sold for about 15¢ per square mile.

The first major upheaval in the life of the community came during the War of Independence. In June 1780, British troops and Hessian mercenaries tried to advance to Morristown, where General George Washington's Continental troops were encamped, by way of Connecticut Farms.

The British and Hessians unexpectedly met a force of local militia and regular Continentals at the village, and, after a fiercely contested battle, withdrew to Staten Island. During their retreat, they burned the village, along with the local Presbyterian church and surrounding farmhouses. No photographs exist from these times, obviously. I had to rely upon the imaginations of several artists for my visual fragments.

Residents rebuilt their houses, and the rest of their village. In 1808, they changed the name of their community—it had become a small town by then—from Connecticut Farms to Union. But the name was just about all that changed. The town remained basically the same, small and rural, well into the twentieth century. Union was very much an out-of-the-way farm town.

The rural character of the town should be very evident from the pictures. In 1940, only about half of Union's roads were paved; the other half were dirt roads. Old-time residents told me that they would sometimes look out of their kitchen windows and see a cow from a nearby farm grazing in their back garden, and that the cows of Green Lane Farm regularly stopped traffic on Morris Avenue by wandering into the street.

But the town's second disruption had already begun to leave its mark. The automobile changed Union from a farming community to a commuting town. By the 1960s, very few Union residents worked in town, let alone on farms. As time went by, fewer and fewer people shopped in Union, as well.

After the Second World War, the town began to develop from a small suburb into a segment of northern New Jersey's swarming urban sprawl. Photographs from many sources illustrate this change, like the fragments of a mosaic. Whether or not the change is for better or worse is up to the reader—or viewer—to decide. This photo-history began in London in the spring of 1994, when friends asked if I would like to do such a project. During the next several months, I copied photographs, assembled pictures, wrote captions, and tried to keep the goal of the project in sight throughout the process.

I hope the book as a whole, as well as by its many individual photographs, will entertain, give an idea of how life looked not all that long ago, and possibly even give pause for reflection.

These fragments I have shored against my ruins.

D.A. Johnson
Union, New Jersey, USA
Brentford, Middlesex, England

One

"Give 'em Watts"

This marker outside the churchyard of Connecticut Farms Church gives a thumbnail history of the town's early days. When this photograph was shown to people in England, they objected to the word "invasion," since New Jersey was still a British colony during the War of Independence. The name was changed to Union in 1808, not 1880, as erroneously stated on the sign.

A painting of the Battle of Connecticut Farms on June 6, 1780. The Continentals (Americans) and local militia are in the foreground; British regulars are in the distance. To the right is the Presbyterian church. Although the British did not succeed in advancing to Morristown, which was their objective, they drove the locals and Continentals from the field and burnt the town.

Among the buildings destroyed by the retreating British was Connecticut Farms Presbyterian Church. In this painting, done nearly two hundred years after the event, General George Washington, Baron von Steuben, and the Marquis de Lafayette inspect the ruins of the church.

Reverend James Caldwell, in a portrait painted during the early twentieth century. Reverend Caldwell was pastor of Elizabeth Town Presbyterian Church and also served as deputy quartermaster general of the Continental Army. (First Presbyterian Church, Elizabeth, NJ)

A statue of Reverend James Caldwell. He was known as "The Fighting Parson" by the Continental Army and the local militia, and as "The Rebel High Priest" by the British. Reverend Caldwell was shot and killed by an American guard named James Morgan on November 24, 1781. Morgan was tried for murder, found guilty, and hanged on Gallows Hill in Westfield. (Presbyterian Historical Society, Philadelphia, PA)

Three romantic views of Reverend Caldwell at the Battle of Springfield on June 23, 1780, to illustrate an equally romantic legend. During the battle, Continental troops began to run out of paper wadding for their muskets. According to the story, Reverend Caldwell took an armful of Isaac Watts' hymnals from the Springfield Presbyterian Church and gave them to the troops, tearing pages from them for musket wads. "Give 'em Watts, boys," he told the troops. "Put Watts into them." (UTHS)

15

Hannah Caldwell, the wife of Reverend James Caldwell, was killed by a shot fired through the window of the parsonage. A short while later, the parsonage was set alight by British troops and burnt to the ground. All of this took place on June 7, 1780, during the Battle of Connecticut Farms. British officers claimed that Mrs. Caldwell had been killed by a Continental (American) soldier, but local troops were convinced that the shooting had been done by the British. The death of Mrs. Caldwell became such a part of local folklore that the scene was adopted as the official seal of Union County. (UTHS)

The Caldwell parsonage, which was built on the foundation of the house that was burnt in 1780. Even in 1900, it was known as "The Old Parsonage." This postcard dates from the turn of the century. (UTHS)

The parsonage in the late 1940s, when it was still a private residence. It was built in 1782, and served as the home of the pastor of Connecticut Farms Church until the early 1900s. In 1960 it became a museum, and is open to the public. (UTHS)

Battle Lines Form Again At Caldwell Parsonage

By EDGAR BROWNE

Union Township's historic Caldwell Parsonage, the site of one of the state's most heroic Revolutionary War incidents, is now the center of a civil war.

On one side are the 200 enthusiastic historians of the Union township Historical Society, who plan to open as a public museum, the three-story frame house they recently purchased, at 909 Caldwell Ave.

On the other side, are residents of the area, who say the museum would impair property values and increase traffic on the already congested Caldwell Ave. They plan to defend their area as vigorously as did Revolutionary War heroine, Hannah Caldwell, the parson's wife. She gave

Albert L. Simpson

Union County Seal depicts tragedy at Caldwell Parsonage.

her life defending the parsonage on June 7, 1780 against marauding Hessians retreating from the Battle of Springfield.

Theme of County Seal

Idealized as one of the county's most cherished heroines, Hannah was the wife of the "fighting parson," Rev. James Caldwell of the Elizabeth Presbyterian Church, who left his wife and brood at the parsonage in Connecticut farms, as union was then known, while he fought alongside the Continentals.

The slaying of Mrs. Caldwell has been emblazoned in bronze on the seal of Union County.

A mural in the County Court House shows Parson Caldwell tearing up hymn books to use the pages as musket wadding.

The congregation of the Connecticut Farms Presbyterian Church rebuilt the parsonage in 1782 on the old foundations and it was used as a home for min-

isters until the early 1900s when it was sold for a residence.

Organized two years ago by Albert Simpson, who is now president, and Louis J. Giacona, Union township building inspector, the historical society raised $17,000 by public subscription to buy the parsonage.

Opposed by Neighbors

Announcement of plans to renovate the parsonage and open it as a museum brought protest from 35 owners of neighboring property. A suit to block public use in a residential zone was started.

"If the society is prevented from operating the museum, steps will be taken to turn it over to the township or state," said Simpson.

The Rev. Fred W. Druckenmiller, present pastor of the Connecticut Farms Presbyterian Church, is chairman for the dedication of the building on June 7 the 180th anniversary of the burning of the original parsonage.

The historical society is collecting contemporary furniture and other Revolutionary War relics to stock the museum.

In 1958, Governor Robert Meyer signed a document proclaiming the week of September 20–26, 1959, as "Save the Caldwell Parsonage Week." The parsonage was saved; the story is given in the news story at left. Below, a plaque gives a short history of the house. (UTHS)

NEAR THIS SPOT
STOOD THE PARSONAGE IN WHICH
HANNAH OGDEN
WIFE OF
REV. JAMES CALDWELL
WAS KILLED BY A BRITISH SOLDIER,
JUNE 7, 1780.

ERECTED BY
THE STATE OF NEW JERSEY
A.D. 1905

The interior of the Caldwell parsonage in 1994. Although renovated to the Colonial style, the parsonage contains artifacts and photographs from every era in Union's past. Over the mantle is the painting of the Battle of Connecticut Farms seen on page 10.

Two

First Families,
Old Homesteads

An engaging portrait of the Beach family. About 1870, Mr. Beach was an elder of Connecticut Farms Church and served on the Township Committee. (UTHS)

Among the original settlers of Connecticut Farms was the Miller family. This is George Miller, looking every bit the Victorian gentleman, about 1880. (UTHS)

The Miller house, on Colonial Avenue near Chestnut Street, is one of the oldest houses in Union. It has been the home of the Miller family since it was built in 1730. (UTHS)

Another landholding clan was the Woodruff family. This is an engraving of Noah Woodruff from about 1860. (UTHS)

Woodruff House, Conant Avenue (now Hillside), built in the 1700s. Hillside was originally known as Lyons Farms, and was a part of Union until 1913. (UTHS)

Elmwood Avenue, about 1890. This is Abner Headley's farm, which extended from Elmwood Avenue to Morris Avenue. The farmhouse is on the right; on the left side of the photograph are stables. (UTHS)

The Headleys were among the original settlers of Union. Leonard Headley, who lived in Connecticut Farms in the early 1700s, was a weaver and owned a sawmill. This is James Headley, with his wife and children, about 1900. (UTHS)

John B. Bonnell and son on their farm, at the corner of Stuyvesant Avenue and Roosevelt Avenue, about 1915. Union was still predominantly open farm country, even this close to Union Center. (UTHS)

Some descendants of the Bonnell family of Connecticut, who settled the land outside of Elizabethtown in the early 1700s. This is the Bonnell family in 1945, shortly after the end of the Second World War. Harvey Bonnell, second from the left, served in the US Army. (UTHS)

Another family that lived in Union since before the War of Independence was the Burnets. The Burnet family posed for this photograph about 1890. (UTHS)

Daniel Burnet, a schoolteacher, in a photograph from about 1850. (UTHS)

Another member of the Burnet family—Edward Burnet, with very stylish mutton chops, about 1875. (UTHS)

Mrs. Aaron Burnet, in a photograph from about 1875. (UTHS)

The homestead of the Stiles Dairy Farm, on Morris Avenue southwest of Colonial Avenue. The house dates from about 1800. (UTHS)

One of Union's grand old farmhouses—a twenty-room house on Peter and Barbara Ernst's dairy farm in a photograph from 1912. It was situated roughly where Balmoral Avenue is today; the street in front is Stuyvesant Avenue. It was pulled down in 1925. Seated on the porch is a young May Ash. (UTHS)

The Blue House, built on the Kean estate (near Kean College) before 1800. (UTHS)

In 1988, the Blue House was moved inside the Liberty Hall complex on Morris Avenue. (UTHS)

The Haines were early settlers of Union. For many years they owned a produce and garden shop on Washington Avenue. (The shop is now on display in the Smithsonian Institution in Washington, DC.) This portrait of the Haines family dates from about 1870. (UTHS)

An unidentified member of the Lum family, about 1870. The Lums owned large tracts of land in the vicinity of Salem Road. (UTHS)

Three

The Center

"The Cannon" at the intersection of Elmwood Avenue and Stuyvesant Avenue, about 1905. The manse of Connecticut Farms Church is the house just beyond the cannon, and the churchyard's monuments can be seen between the trees on Stuyvesant Avenue. The gun itself dates from the War of Independence, but the carriage is from the Civil War. (UT)

Ye Olde Meeker Inn, on Morris Avenue, near Stuyvesant Avenue. The inn was standing during the War of Independence, but avoided destruction because it was not along the route of march of either army. This postcard is postmarked 1909—postage: 1¢. (Clem Johnson)

The Meeker Inn in 1925. It had became an insurance agency by this time, as well as a fruit and vegetable market and a shoe repair shop. The inn was pulled down in 1930, and is now the site of the Union Center National Bank. By the 1920s, Union Center was becoming more commercial, although much of the town remained undeveloped farmland. (UTHS)

The Union Center National Bank, in a photograph from 1947. The bank's well-known lighted clock/thermometer had not yet been installed above the main entrance. (Millicent Egbert)

Three young dandies pose in front of Ye Olde Meeker Inn with their Model T Ford. Cars have never been the same since Detroit discontinued rumble seats and running boards. (UT)

Old post office is down the road apiece

A television antenna sprouts where the roof once sloped; the store windows have been replaced by an entranceway flanked by a pair of columns, and even the site is different.

But the building shown in the picture which recently was presented to the Township Committee still stands—and not far from its original location.

Donated to the township by May Ong, the photo shows the structure which at one time stood at the Union Center site now occupied by Kodak Jewelers: a sturdy brick building, with a general store and post office on the ground floor, and bay-windowed apartments above.

A half a century ago, Edwin Patterson, who owned the building, found a new location for it at 1939 Morris ave.

"We just put it on rollers and moved it," said Patterson, who now lives in Watchung. There was no problem," he recalled.

Its sloping roof replaced by a flat one, the building still serves as a six-family apartment house.

There were apartments upstairs when the building was at its old location, but the first floor served a variety of purposes. It was not only general store and post office, Patterson said; it also served as police headquarters for a time in the 1920s, when Charles Hopkins was chief. And at one time there was a gas station there as well, he added.

Patterson has good reason to remember. His mother, Jessie May Patterson, born Fink, was postmistress at the time.

Her people had homesteaded in Connecticut Farms, and on Oct. 4, 1899, Jessie May Fink of Union and Robert J. Patterson of Roselle were married in the Caldwell Parsonage, now a museum.

Years later, Patterson presented the ornate wedding certificate to the Caldwell Parsonage Museum along with other family papers, including his mother's appointment as postmaster, dated Dec. 28, 1920.

(Clem Johnson)

34

(Clem Johnson)

(Clem Johnson)

John O. Price's General Merchandise and Groceries, around 1925. The shop was built by the grandfather of Clem Johnson, who submitted this photograph. At various times, it served as a welfare station (during the Depression), police headquarters, and post office. (Clem Johnson)

The intersection of Morris Avenue and Stuyvesant Avenue, about 1914. By this time, the gasoline buggy was more in evidence—note the man standing next to the gasoline pump in the center of the photograph. The building is the Union General Store and Post Office. Stuyvesant Avenue is the street on the left. (UT)

Stuyvesant Avenue in 1910, still a dirt road. This view is from Elmwood Avenue's cannon looking toward Morris Avenue. (UT)

This is another view of what the Center looked like at the turn of the century—a few buildings surrounded by open fields. The park at the intersection of Stuyvesant Avenue and Elmwood Avenue was known as "The Triangle" when this photograph was taken c. 1900. (UTHS)

Stuyvesant Avenue around 1900, looking from Roosevelt Avenue toward Connecticut Farms Church. At the extreme left, just above the first fence post, is Connecticut Farms School; visible above the roof of the school is the cupola of the Town Hall. Beyond the trees, hidden from view, is Connecticut Farms Church; visible to the right of the clump of trees is the church's cemetary. (CF)

Another view of Stuyvesant Avenue in the 1890s. The exact location is unidentified. From the photograph, it can be seen that Union was still very rural—the population was under three thousand at this time. (CF)

Union High School's football team calls itself "The Farmers." But at the turn of the century, many Unionites were working farmers. This photograph was taken around 1900. In the background are the buildings of Union Center. (UT)

Union's first post office was located inside the Westbake General Store on West Chestnut Street near Stuyvesant Avenue. This scene, from about 1907, gives another indication of the rural character of the town. Painting by K.C. Smith.

The Falls Building, on the corner of Morris and Stuyvesant Avenues, about 1925. The Union Center National Bank is the shop in front of the car; it would not move to its current location for another five years. Union's one and only cinema does not yet have a marquee, and Morris Avenue has not yet been paved. (Neither has Stuyvesant Avenue.) In the dozen years since the end of the First World War, Union had developed from a country village to a growing suburban town—with growing commerce, a growing population, and increased traffic. (UT)

"Bread is Fightin' Food!" reads the sign atop the Falls Building—the photograph dates from the Second World War era. Whelans Drugs occupies the building's main shop, and all of the roads are paved. The Center had expanded since the 1920s, and so had the town itself. In the years following the war, the town would change and expand still further. (Mrs. Jack Zissel)

The corner of Morris Avenue and Stuyvesant Avenue in 1942. Lerner Department Store, Shoes and Dry Goods was just next door to the Union Center National Bank. (UTHS)

In the 1930s, Union still had mounted police; these five are parading on Stuyvesant Avenue. The building on the right is near the intersection of Rosemont Avenue. (Union Police)

Union Center during the Second World War. The marquee of the Union Cinema urges the public to "Buy War Bonds." Unfortunately, the feature film is not listed. An Acme supermarket is on the left side of Stuyvesant Avenue. All shopping, from food to clothing, could be done in the Center—which was especially useful at the time because of travel restrictions imposed by wartime gasoline rationing. (Mrs. Jack Zissel)

Morris Avenue at the Center, about 1944. The DeLuxe Diner, home of the DeLuxe hamburger, is in the center of the photograph. Next to the diner is a one-pump Sinclair gasoline station; next to the station is a vacant lot, which had been the site of the Union General Store and Post Office. (Mrs. Jack Zissel)

Looking toward Elizabeth from Friberger Park, about 1930, over a quarter of a century before the Municipal Building was built. The first line of houses is Grandview Avenue; just beyond is Floyd Terrace, then Ingersoll Terrace. Morris Avenue is the roadway to the left, just beyond the thicket of trees. (UT)

When the post office and general store was moved from the corner of Stuyvesant Avenue and Morris Avenue, it was given a new home a short distance away on Morris Avenue. This site is just a few doors down from the Union Center National Bank. (Mrs. Jack Zissel)

Morris Avenue at Stuyvesant Avenue on a summer day in the early 1950s. On the corner is Fields Jewelers; just down the street is Kless' Diner, formerly the DeLuxe Diner. (UT)

Stuyvesant Avenue shops in 1947. The building at the extreme left, which houses the Singer sewing machine shop and the Thrift Shop, had just been built. (Millicent Egbert)

Morris Avenue, in a photograph taken from the Sinclair gasoline station. The building housing Perkins Pharmacy, formerly the site of the general store and post office, had been built in 1947. (Millicent Egbert)

In the early 1950s, 3-D movies were all the rage. The audience wore special glasses, with cardboard frames, one red lens, and one green lens—this was supposed to make the images on screen seem completely lifelike. The fad ran its course fairly quickly, thankfully. A semi-reliable source reports that *Charge at Feather River* dates from 1953. (UT)

Stuyvesant Avenue in 1953. Now playing at the Union Cinema: *Shane*, starring Alan Ladd. (UT)

The Elmwood Avenue cannon in the 1950s. The traffic sign points the way to the Garden State Parkway ramps. (UT)

The Center in the 1970s. It had come a long way, for better or worse, since the dirt-road-and-trolley-tracks days of before the Second World War. Business was booming, but life was more hectic and the town was more crowded. This photograph shows a rare moment when traffic was light at the intersection of Morris Avenue and Stuyvesant Avenue. (UTHS)

CONN. FARMS 1900
AT THE CENTER

A painting of the Center in 1900. The building on the left is Ye Olde Meeker Inn. The painting now hangs on the upper floor of the Town Hall.

Four

Death and Taxes and Politics and Politicians

In 1942, a few months after the Pearl Harbor attack, Mayor F. Edward Biertuempfel (second from the right) and other town officials pose in Friberger Park with the air raid wardens and equipment of Civil Defense Unit No. 2. (UTHS)

Union Town Hall about 1900, when it occupied the site of the present Connecticut Farms School. It was too hot in summer, too cold in winter, and altogether uncomfortable as an office building. (UT)

Another view of the Town Hall, taken about 1914. The little girl in the foreground is Anne Rhymer. She is standing in front of Connecticut Farms Church, and, judging from her clothes, she was photographed either just before or just after Sunday school, possibly by her father. Stuyvesant Avenue was still a rutted dirt road at this point. (UT)

Friberger Park before the Municipal Building was built on the site. This photograph dates from 1943, when the population of Union Township was about twenty-five thousand. The lot, which had been known as the Hoyt estate, was acquired by the Township in 1938. (UT)

Union's Municipal Building in 1957, shortly after it was opened. Prior to these new offices, the Township Committee met in various places, including the Falls Building, the Civic Center (next to Connecticut Farms School), and the Meeker Inn. (UT)

Before Friberger Park became Union's municipal center, Connecticut Farms held that distinction. Across Stuyvesant Avenue from Connecticut Farms Church are the Union Fire Department (center), Union Town Hall (right), and the old Connecticut Farms School (left). The original photograph is captioned "circa 1918," but the car parked in back of the school is of a much later vintage. (UT)

Another view of the Town Hall and Connecticut Farms School (left), during the winter of 1900. (CF)

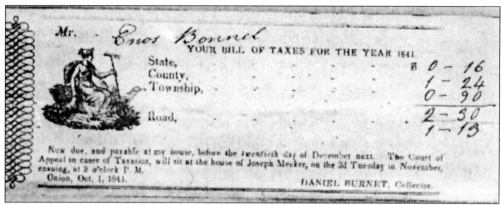

Enos Bonnel's tax bill from October 1841. Township tax was 90¢. Mr. Bonnel probably complained bitterly about the high cost of living in Union. (UT)

Even in the early 1800s, there was no escape from taxes and licensing fees. This carriage certificate was issued to Daniel Sayers on January 31, 1815, when James Madison was president of the United States. The fee was $2; the vehicle was "a two wheel carriage, called a chair." (UTHS)

A 1945 photograph of Morris Avenue, just down the street from the Union Center National Bank. The funeral procession of I.D. Harris, Union's first postmaster, passes in front of the Union Post Office. Above the post office is the selective service board—it was wartime, and the draft was still in effect. (UT)

F. Edward Biertuempfel was mayor of Union from 1939 until his death in 1973. He had been a member of the Township Committee since 1930. When he first came to Union, the town was small and rural; by the time of his death, it had become much more urban. Biertuempfel probably had more of an impact on Union than any other single person. This photograph dates from the 1940s. (UT)

One of the last photographs of Mayor Biertuempfel, taken on January 1, 1973. Standing behind him are Township Committeemen James Conlon, Anthony E. Russo, Samuel Rabkin, John Yacovelle, and Township Clerk Mary E. Miller. (UT)

The Dewey for President Club, at the corner of Morris Avenue and Johnson Place, in the summer of 1948. Mayor Biertuempfel stands to the left of Thomas Dewey's portrait. Although Dewey had been picked to win the presidential election that year, he did not have quite enough votes to unseat incumbent Harry S. Truman. (UT)

Biertuempfel dutifully campaigned for Republican candidates throughout his tenure as mayor. Here, he poses with Republican officials during Richard Nixon's unsuccessful campaign for the presidency in 1960. (UTHS)

"COPS NAB RACKETEERS" seems a likely caption for this photograph. Actually, the sinister-looking gents seated in the foreground are Union's distinguished Township Committee: Charles A. Barber, Max A. Schoenwalder, Ambrose B. Kune (mayor), Gustav Hummel, and William Honrath. Among the policemen is Jacob Denk (fifth from the right), who later became police chief. This photograph dates from December 28, 1928. (UT)

During the Second World War, everybody wanted to get involved in the war effort. Some of those who were exempted from military service volunteered as auxiliary police. In this 1943 photograph, auxiliaries pose in front of the old police headquarters on Caldwell Avenue. The civilians are: (left to right) Committeeman Harry E. King, Mayor F. Edward Biertuempfel, and Committeeman Robert R. Lackey. (UT)

On April 13, 1989, President George Bush visited Union High School during his single term in office. Here, he addresses the audience in the school's auditorium; to his right is New Jersey Governor Thomas Kean. (UT)

Five

Unwillingly to School

A photograph from the late 1890s, when Union only had one school. Third from the left is Mary Ernst, the daughter of Peter Ernst. Mary eventually married Ed Ash; her daughter, May, donated this photograph to Union Township. (UT)

The corncrib on the Stiles Dairy Farm on Morris Avenue. The photograph is undated; it could date as far back as the 1860s. This building possibly served as one of Union's earliest schoolhouses; all grades and all classes were taught in a single room. (UTHS)

Connecticut Farms School kids in May 1889. By this time, Union had come a long way from the one-room schoolhouse, but still needed only one school. (CF)

The lull before the storm. Grammar school children at Connecticut Farms School pose quietly, with hands neatly folded, in the 1920s. But the clock on the back wall indicates that lunch will begin in twenty minutes—at which time all hell will break loose. (UT)

The inmates of Connecticut Farms School pose in back of the school building in 1888. Just beyond the fence, visible to the right of the building, is Stuyvesant Avenue. (CF)

"Vaux Hall School" in the mid-1920s, in a photograph contributed by Clem Johnson. Mr. Johnson's aunt, Gertrude Johnson, taught this class. (Clem Johnson)

This photograph is a bit earlier than the one above. Although no date is given, the reverse of the photograph has the inscription: "The first class Grandma ever taught; Gertrude Johnson, Teacher, Vaux Hall School." (Clem Johnson)

Teacher's Record

Name _Gertrude Johnson_ 3 Race St. Date of Birth _Apr. 18, 1896_ Place of Birth _Kingston,_
Permanent Home Address _828 So. Orange Ave._ _Hillside_ _Newark, N. J._ Nationality _America_

Year	City Address	Phone No.	Year	City Address	Phone No.

Certificates: Kind _State Per._ Date _1915_ By whom issued _State_ Renewed .... Expires ....

Grade of Work Preferred ....

Teaching Experience in Local Schools

Year	Building	Position (Make Clear)	Yearly Salary	Days Absent	Year	Building	Position (Make Clear)	Yearly Salary	Days Absent
1915	Vaux Hall	2nd.	550						
1916	"	"	"	600					
1917	"	"	"	650					
1918	"	"	"	675					
1920	"	"	"	800					
1921	"	"	"	1100					
1922	"	"	"	1250					
1923	"	"	"	1250					
1924	"	"	"	1250					

STRAYER-ENGELHARDT SCHOOL RECORD CARD SERIES—C. F. WILLIAMS & SON, INC., ALBANY, N. Y.   (OV)

"Nobody ever became a teacher for the money" was as true in the early part of this century as it ever was. This is the teacher's record of Gertrude Johnson, from 1915 to 1924, at Vaux Hall School. She started at $550 per year. After nine years, she was earning $1,250 per year. (Clem Johnson)

Public Schools, Union County, N. J.

Certificate of Merit.

Awarded to _Clement Johnson_ a Pupil in
the District of _Connecticut Farms_ Primary Grade
as a Testimonial for having passed all the requirements for that
Grade; also for regular attendance, correct deportment and diligent
attention.   Elizabeth, N. J., _June 11th,_ 1903.

Lottie B Griggs Teacher   _D. H. Beach_ Dist. Clerk.
Andrew B. Vliet, Principal. W. J. Shearer, County Supt.

A certificate awarded to Clement Johnson, "a pupil in the district of Connecticut Farms," on June 11, 1903. (Clem Johnson)

A very mature-looking class of graduating eighth graders assembled for a photograph on June 21, 1916. The girls wore all white, including shoes and gloves; the boys were turned out in suits and stiff celluloid collars. The dour-looking gent with the moustache is Ambrose B. Kline, a stern, no-nonsense principal. (UT)

One of the early graduating classes of Union High School, probably about 1886. In the 1880s, a formal education seldom went beyond grammar school: a high school diploma was considered unnecessary for running a farm. For their graduation photograph, these five outgoing seniors dressed up in their Sunday finery, complete with hair ribbons and celluloid collars. (UT)

A graduating class of Connecticut Farms School, sometime in the 1880s. From their expressions, the students look as though they expect to be shot by a firing squad, instead of by a photographer. (CF)

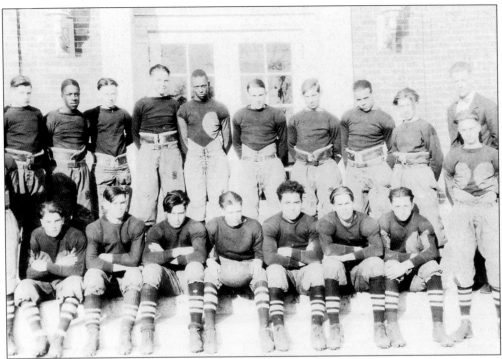

Union High School's football team poses on the steps in front of the school in the autumn of 1925. (UTHS)

The new Connecticut Farms Grammar School in the mid-1940s. Union's population was growing, and the old school had become outdated. Its teachers would have said that it had become decrepit. (Mrs. Jack Zissel)

Before Kean College, there was Newark State College. Before Newark State College, there was Green Lane Farm. In this photograph, taken in 1935, cows drink from a trough in front of the grandly ornate farmhouse. Cows frequently disrupted traffic on Morris Avenue while crossing from one side to the other. In the early 1950s the state of New Jersey acquired the land and in 1958 Newark State Teachers College moved to the site. Union residents still debate whether or not college students represent an improvement over cows. (UT)

The farmhouse, photographed about thirty-five years later, and its well-known tower. The building has been used in many capacities, including as a library and as administrative offices. Its tower was incorporated into the college seal (left).

A familiar sight on the corner of Morris Avenue and Caldwell Avenue was Union High School's cannon. The cannon is a German 105mm howitzer which was captured during the First World War. This photograph dates from 1942, but the scene looked the same until the high school moved across town in 1969. Although the cannon belonged on its concrete slab in front of the school, it was sometimes manhandled into the middle of Morris Avenue by graduating seniors as a farewell gesture to dear old alma mater. (Millicent Egbert)

Six

The Heart of the Community

Connecticut Farms Church was not only the spiritual center of Union—it was the only church in town until 1873—it was also the social center for many decades. This photograph dates from the early 1900s, but the scene probably looked the same a hundred years before. (CF)

Looking up the hill from West Chestnut Street, about 1910. This is an unusual photograph of the church, and gives a good view of the original building. Across the street is the Town Hall, and between the church and the Town Hall, the old Connecticut Farms School. The building to the right of the Town Hall is Union Jail. No sidewalks are in evidence, and roads are just two-wheel ruts. Among the social events that were held in Connecticut Farms Church were school graduation exercises. Any events that were pronounced "unsuitable," or were too large to be held inside the church, were moved to the Town Hall. (UT)

Connecticut Farms Church and churchyard during the Second World War, before the addition was built in 1949. When the church was enlarged, the graves situated in back of the church—including those of some Hessian soldiers killed in the fighting of 1780—were moved. (Mrs. Jack Zissel)

A print of Connecticut Farms Church. Judging from the style of dress, it dates from about 1840. (CF)

The manse—home of the pastor—in an early, undated print. (CF)

The Caldwell parsonage on Caldwell Avenue was still used as the pastor's residence until the early years of the twentieth century. The elderly man in the straw boater is Reverend Robert Street. The photograph is undated, but Reverend Street resigned as pastor in 1886. (CF)

Reverend Street, along with his wife and daughter, relaxing in the parsonage's front garden, sometime in the 1880s. (CF)

The Ladies Aid Society of Connecticut Farms Church posed for the photographer in their white cotton frocks in 1911. The man in the dark suit is Reverend Almer Karnall, who had been installed as pastor in 1900. (CF)

A skit performed at Connecticut Farms Church, *Sewing Circle Meets at Mrs. Martins*, in 1929. The performance was probably part of the annual Peach Festival, which later became the church's well-known Strawberry Festival. (CF)

Reverend Robert Street was pastor of Connecticut Farms Church for fifty years, from 1836 to 1886. In the years before the Civil War, Reverend Street was known for his anti-slavery views: this opinion caused many members to leave the church. (CF)

Reverend Fred Druckenmiller, pastor from 1928 to 1962. When he arrived, the population of Union was fourteen thousand; when he resigned, it was over fifty thousand. During his pastorate, Union endured the depths of the Great Depression of the 1930s and enjoyed the prosperity of the post-war boom years. (CF)

Looking across Stuyvesant Avenue at Connecticut Farms Church, around 1880. At the time, the building was about a hundred years old. It was rebuilt by the year 1788, on the same site as its predecessor, which had been destroyed during the War of Independence. (UT)

A scene taken across the street from Connecticut Farms Church, on Wewanna Avenue, about 1890. The horse and wagon are parked in front of the post office. Although a few daredevils rode bicycles, the primary method of transportation was still the horse, with or without a buggy. (UT)

Connecticut Farms Church in 1944, as seen from the Memorial Park on Wewanna Avenue, not far from the scene on the preceding page. An addition, the "parish house," has already been built; it is visible behind the thick line of trees to the left. A more extensive wing would be added in 1949. Among the Township officials are Esther Egbert, the mother-in-law of the photograph's contributor, and Mayor Biertuempfel, who is standing at Mrs. Egbert's right shoulder. (Millicent Egbert)

After 192 years of wear and weather, the church's sagging 15-ton steeple was removed in 1983 for major renovation. The steeple was completely rebuilt and replaced in 1985. It is still a town landmark, as it has been since 1791. (CF)

Seven

Get a Horse!

At the turn of the century, a person could get away with almost anything as long as he remembered not to frighten the horses. No one remembers what W.L. Edwards delivered, but his faithful stallion seems quite composed, in spite of the presence of an intrusive camera. (UT)

Morris Turnpike—now Morris Avenue—in 1896, when it was a narrow dirt path. The site of the photograph is near the entrance to Suburban Golf Club, in the vicinity of Sayre Road. Morris Turnpike, which ran from Elizabethtown to Springfield and Morristown, was New Jersey's first toll road. It brought travellers through Connecticut Farms, many of whom stopped at the Meeker Inn for a meal and a drink before continuing on. (UT)

The gas man cometh. An Elizabethtown gas vehicle c. 1890, advertising gas ranges and gas heaters for homes. Gas appliances were the latest thing in those days—a lot more convenient than the old wood-burning stoves, and safer than kerosene lamps. (UTHS)

The intersection of Morris Avenue and Stuyvesant Avenue, about 1920. On the left is Ye Olde Meeker Inn; in the center is the general store and post office. Automobiles still shared the road with horses. The young fellow with the horse doesn't seem very concerned about holding up traffic on Morris Avenue, but that doesn't seem to matter, since the only car in the photograph isn't going anywhere. (UT)

An open touring car on Springfield Avenue, about 1906. This horseless carriage was meant for daytime driving only—it has no headlights—and for fair-weather motoring. These restrictions kept the horse in the lead as the preferred method of travel until the time of the First World War, when Henry Ford introduced the Model T. (Marguerite Miltner)

Rush-hour traffic on Morris Avenue, c. 1900. The two cyclists pass in front of Ye Olde Meeker Inn; note the wagon wheel ruts in the dusty shoulder of the road. The street sign behind the cyclist on the right marks the intersection with Stuyvesant Avenue. No other buildings, or traffic, can be seen in this photograph—Union was still very much a farm town. (CF)

J.E. Miller delivering milk. This photograph was taken near the Lehigh Valley Railroad crossing in Roselle Park, sometime in the 1920s. (UT)

An amateur photographer took this photograph of traffic on North Avenue at the intersection of Morris Avenue about 1890. Note the narrowness of the street. (UT)

Two views of Morris Avenue and Salem Road about 1945. The top photograph looks north on Salem Road toward Hillside; the bottom is Morris Avenue, looking toward Elizabeth. (Mrs. Jack Zissel)

Two views of Highway 29, now Route 22, in the mid-1940s. The top photograph was taken in front of the Garden State Motor Lodge; Hi-Way Bowl is on the other side of the highway. The bottom photograph shows the same view, as seen from the Vauxhall Road overpass; the Garden State Motor Lodge is on the left. Traffic on the highway is so light that it is almost non-existent, which says a lot about life in and around Union, and about the pace of life at the time. Union was no longer a farm town, but it was still very much a suburb; it had not yet become a part of the New York Metropolitan Area sprawl. (Mrs. Jack Zissel)

The trolley that ran from Elizabeth through Union to Springfield and points beyond, pictured on Morris Avenue. The photograph dates from 1907 and was possibly taken on the first day of service. The fare is not recorded, but it is remembered that holdups were not infrequent along this line. (UT)

The Burnet Avenue trolley, about the same time as the photograph on the opposite page. Burnet Avenue consisted of two very narrow dirt lanes, plus trolley tracks. The trolley was thought to be more reliable than the automobile. For one thing, because it ran on tracks, it never got stuck in the mud, and never had a flat tire. (UT)

A delivery wagon stops at the John Doly residence on Elmwood Avenue, sometime around 1898. The deliveryman's helper takes a break, and poses for a picture. (CF)

Horses were not just for riding and for pulling wagons. Frazier Alick handles a plough horse on the Apgar Farm, on Morris Avenue and Apgar Court, in an undated photograph. (UTHS)

What Henry Ford hath wrought. An aerial view of Union in the 1960s, soon after the Union water tower was built. Route 22 and the Garden State Parkway pass over Morris Avenue in an almost endless stream of traffic. The area is not far from the section of the Morris Turnpike shown on page 90. One hundred years before, Union meant the comforts of the Meeker Inn—a drink and a good meal. Now, for many travellers, Union is nothing more than exit 139 or 140 on the Parkway—a town glimpsed through a rolled-up window at 60 miles per hour. The coming of the automobile, and everything that came with it, has been very much a mixed blessing—cars meant increased independence and mobility, but superhighways have taken much of Union's uniqueness away. (UTHS)

Eight

Changing Times

Once the site of the old Connecticut Farms School, the new Civic Center was built as a place for young people to gather—under adult supervision. This photograph dates from the early 1950s. (UTHS)

Swimming on the Kean estate, about 1930. Both men and women wore swimsuits with tops, although a few of the more macho types (left-hand side of the photograph, in the middle of the lake), wore only the bottom. (UT)

An unidentified private residence on Stuyvesant Avenue, about 1890. Barely visible in this faded photograph are, in the right-hand corner, a mounting block (to assist the rider in mounting a horse), and a horse post (for tethering a horse). Henry Ford had not yet made his presence known. (CF)

Sayre Lane in the 1890s, showing Phoebe Sayre's house and farm. The woman getting water in the foreground is Mrs. John Mott. Indoor plumbing was unheard of at this time. (UT)

Another photograph of a Union that is long gone, although not all that long ago. A cow grazes contentedly at the Miller Farm, sometime in the 1920s. Union had at least one active farm as late as the 1960s—the Omara Farm, which was located at the end of Stecher Avenue. (CF)

Artifacts from Union's past. The musket was owned by one James A. Garthwaite of Connecticut Farms, who is said to have used it against the Hessians in 1780. Other items include a fan (1) used in Connecticut Farms Church in summer, and a foot stove (2) used in winter. The small communion set (6) is believed to be the first used in the church. Item (4) is another communion set and the items above the communion sets are boxes for taking collection. (CF)

The original settlers of Connecticut Farms bought their land from the Lenae Lenape Indians at about 15¢ per square mile. These are three arrowheads left by the original inhabitants, shown with a scale to give an idea of their size. (UTHS)

Two young fellows lounge on Tinkettle Hill, about 1890. No one is quite certain just how the hill got its singular name. The site is now Fairway Drive, off Route 22. (CF)

A snowdrift left by the famous—or infamous—blizzard of 1888. The drift is twice as tall as the man in the foreground. Union residents were snowbound for days after the storm; several people actually froze to death in the snow. (UT)

Sleigh-riding down the hill at Friberger Park in the 1800s. (CF)

Union jail and inmates in 1915. The jail was located behind the original Connecticut Farms School. The prisoners are not identified and no living residents of Union have come forward to claim any of those pictured as long-lost relatives. (UT)

Policemen, police cars, and a police dog pose in front of the police headquarters in the 1920s. (UT)

Union's finest pose in front of the Town Hall in the early 1920s. Union was still more of a village than a town; crime was usually of a minor sort, and criminal acts were rare. (UT)

The entire crew of the Vauxhall Volunteer Co. No. 1 turned out to be photographed in their Sunday best on a fine day in the early 1920s. They had spent the morning polishing their lone fire engine. (UT)

Union Fire Brigade in the 1920s—one of its fire engines, a few firemen, and other hangers-on. At the bottom left is Clement Johnson, father of the photograph's contributor. (Clem Johnson)

Union Fire Station on Morris Avenue, near Kean College. This slightly out-of-focus photograph dates from the 1950s. (UTHS)

In the 1970s, another highway ploughed its way through Union. Route 24, Route 22, and the Garden State Parkway had already changed the landscape. The newest interstate would be Route 78. These three photographs show Route 78 under construction in 1978. They were taken in the vicinity of Stanley Terrace; Franklin Elementary School's tower is visible at right in the bottom picture (opposite). (Marguerite Miltner)

Photographs from the Great Depression of the 1930s. The Emergency Employment Relief Bureau was situated two doors down from the Union Cinema, in the former home of the Union Center National Bank. (UT)

The interior of the Emergency Employment office was anything but cheerful and reassuring. (UT)

The Emergency Food Distribution Center was on Haines Avenue, off Chestnut Street. Those in need stood in line for a bag of groceries. Note the horse and wagon, and the unpaved street in the foreground—in 1940, only about half of the Union's streets were paved. (UT)

The inside of the Food Distribution Center. Note that nearly everything there, except for the peas and oranges, are starches and carbohydrates—corn flakes, oats, potatoes, and other basic staples. (UT)

One could dine and dance at the Five Points Restaurant, which later became Petersons and then the Galloping Hill Inn. This photograph is undated, but one of the cars is either a 1940 or a 1941 Plymouth. (UT)

| R - RESTAURANTS (Cont.) | R - RESTAURANTS (Cont.) |

THE
FLAGSHIP

on 29 Highway

DINING
and
DANCING

Entertainment
Nightly

Charles A. Fitze
Prop.

Unvl. 2-3101

Galloping Hill
Inn

Galloping Hill Rd.
and
Chestnut Street

Unvl. 2-2683

Charles L. Hampp
Prop.

NEW CRYSTAL
RESTAURANT

BREAKFASTS
LUNCHEONS
DINNERS

Sandwiches to Order

2039 Springfield Ave.
Unvl. 2-4793

Paul Christopher
Prop.

"BUY IN UNION"

The restaurant page from the 1948 *Union Township Business Directory* features advertisements for the Galloping Hill Inn and The Flagship. (Pauline Foster)

123

DRIVE-IN THEATRE

ROUTE 29 and CHESTNUT ST.   UNION, N. J.

SIT IN YOUR CAR, SEE AND HEAR THE MOVIES

TWO SHOWS NIGHTLY — RAIN OR SHINE

— 35c per Person, No Charge for Car —

An advertisement from the 1938/9 *Union Township Official Guide*.

Back in the 1940s, The Flagship on Highway 29 was a cocktail lounge and restaurant, before the highway was renumbered as Route 22. For 75¢ to $1, one could dine and listen to a live orchestra—drinks were extra. (Mrs. Jack Zissel)

A short while after the top photograph was taken, The Flagship burnt to the ground. Since the 1940s, the building has seen a number of businesses come and go, including the men's clothing shop "American Shops" during the 1950s. (UT)

Schultz's Shell Service Center at Morris Avenue and Colonial Avenue. In the 1940s, Morris Avenue was still paved with concrete, not yet covered with asphalt. (Mrs. Jack Zissel)

Honest Schultz himself. For the price of a tankful of gasoline—about 19¢ per gallon—he checked your tires, battery, radiator, and oil; washed your windshield; gave you trading stamps and free maps; and could even give precise directions. And said "Thank you." (Mrs. Jack Zissel)

In the late 1940s and the 1950s, industry began moving into Union. Allowing "carefully selected" industries into town was part of the plan for Union's expansion. This aerial view shows the early stages in the construction of the Schering Building on Morris Avenue. (UTHS)

In 1977, Union was named an "All-America City": an ideal municipality. In this photograph, residents and officials celebrate the event in front of the Municipal Building. (UTHS)